Hyenas

Victoria Blakemore

For Nina, thank you for sharing your wonderful idea! By the way, it's hyena, not hi Nina! ;)

Copyright info/picture credits

Table of Contents

What Are Hyenas?

Hyenas are mammals. Although they may look like dogs, they are not related to them.

There are three main kinds of hyenas: striped hyenas, spotted hyenas, and brown hyenas. They differ in size and the color of their fur.

Hyenas are usually brown, gray,

black, and red-orange in color.

They can have stripes or spots.

Size

Hyenas can grow to be between about three and six feet long.

When fully grown, they can weigh between about sixty and 180 pounds. Spotted hyenas are the largest kind of hyenas. Striped hyenas are the smallest.

Female spotted hyenas are
usually larger than males.

Physical Characteristics

Hyenas have front legs that are longer than their back legs. They also have thicker muscles in their front legs.

Spotted hyenas have large, rounded ears. Striped hyenas and brown hyenas also have large ears, but theirs are pointed.

Brown hyenas have a coat that is long and thick. The strip of fur down the middle of their back stands up when they are scared.

7

Habitat

Hyenas are able to **adapt** to living in many different habitats. They are often found in deserts, grasslands, swamps, forests, and savannas.

It is usually very hot and dry where hyenas live. Hyenas often jump into watering holes to cool down.

Range

Most hyenas are found in Africa, but some can also be found in parts of Asia.

They are found in countries such as India, Libya, Niger, Algeria, Sudan, and Egypt.

Diet

Hyenas are **carnivores**. They eat only meat. They are known as **scavengers**, which means that they often eat leftovers from other animals' hunting.

Their diet is made up of birds, antelope, wildebeest, hippos, fish, snakes, and other animals.

Hyenas have very strong teeth

and jaws. They are able to crush

bones.

Hyenas work together when they are hunting. Larger groups of hyenas are able to catch larger prey.

After they have caught their prey, hyenas sometimes hide the leftovers near watering holes. They can come back to eat the rest later.

Hyenas eat all parts of animals.

They eat bones, antlers, and

even hooves.

Communication

Hyenas use sound, scent, and movement to communicate with each other. Sounds such as grunts, whoops, and a laughing sound.

They have a special scent that they can use to mark their **territory**. It tells other hyenas to stay away.

Although hyenas are known for their laugh, only spotted hyenas actually make a laughing sound. It is used when they are excited or **anxious.**

17

Movement

Hyenas can run at speeds of up to about thirty-five miles per hour.

They have a lot of **stamina** and can run for long distances.

They have been known to sneak up on prey. They use the color of their fur to hide in long grasses. When prey walks by, they give chase.

Hyenas have a very odd walk. It often looks like they are limping.

This is because their front legs are longer than their back legs. 19

Hyena Cubs

Hyenas usually have a **litter** of between two and four babies. Their babies are called cubs.

When they are first born, cubs are blind. They open their eyes after about a week. Mothers feed their cubs for anywhere between a few months and nearly two years.

Hyena cubs stay with their

mother for about two years.

Then, they are ready to go off

on their own.

Hyena Life

Hyenas are very social animals.

They live in groups that are

called clans. A clan can be

made up of over 100 hyenas.

Spotted hyena clans are run

by the females. They are more

aggressive than the males.

With brown hyenas and striped

hyenas, the opposite is true.

Clans work together to hunt.

Some clans also help each

other to take care of cubs.

Aardwolves

Although aardwolves may sound like they are wolves, they are not wolves. They are from the same family as hyenas.

Unlike hyenas, aardwolves do not hunt large animals. They eat mainly insects and their larvae.

Aardwolves are only found in Africa. They are **nocturnal** and are rarely seen during the day.

Population

Although hyenas are not currently **endangered**, their populations have been **declining**.

The spotted hyena is listed as **least concern**. The striped hyena, brown hyena, and aardwolf are all **near threatened**.

In the wild, hyenas often live

between ten and twelve years.

In zoos, they usually live longer.

Hyenas in Danger

Hyenas in the wild are facing several large threats. Most of their threats come from living near people.

In many places, hyenas are thought to be **pests** because they feed on **livestock**. Many farmers trap or kill hyenas to keep their animals safe.

Hyena habitats are being destroyed. They are being cleared for buildings, roads, and farms.

Helping Hyenas

Although hyenas are often thought of as dangerous **pests**, many people are trying to help them.

In some places, hyenas live in special protected areas. These protected areas provide animals like hyenas with safe habitats.

Some groups work with farmers in areas where hyenas are found. They help the farmers to build special **enclosures** to protect their **livestock**.

Other groups focus on research and education. They want to learn more about hyenas so they can find new ways to help them.

Glossary

Adapt: to change or adjust

Aggressive: mean, ready to fight

Anxious: feeling worried or afraid

Carnivore: an animal that eats only meat

Declining: getting smaller

Enclosure: a space that is surrounded by a fence or wall

Endangered: at risk of becoming extinct

Least concern: when an animal is not at risk of becoming endangered

Livestock: animals such as chickens, cows, or sheep that are kept on farms

Near threatened: when an animal could become endangered if the population continues to decline

Nocturnal: most active at night

Pests: someone or something that annoys or bothers

Scavenger: an animal that eats dead animals or plants

Stamina: the strength to handle long effort

About the Author

Victoria Blakemore is a first grade

teacher in Southwest Florida with a

passion for reading.

You can visit her at

www.elementaryexplorers.com

Also in This Series

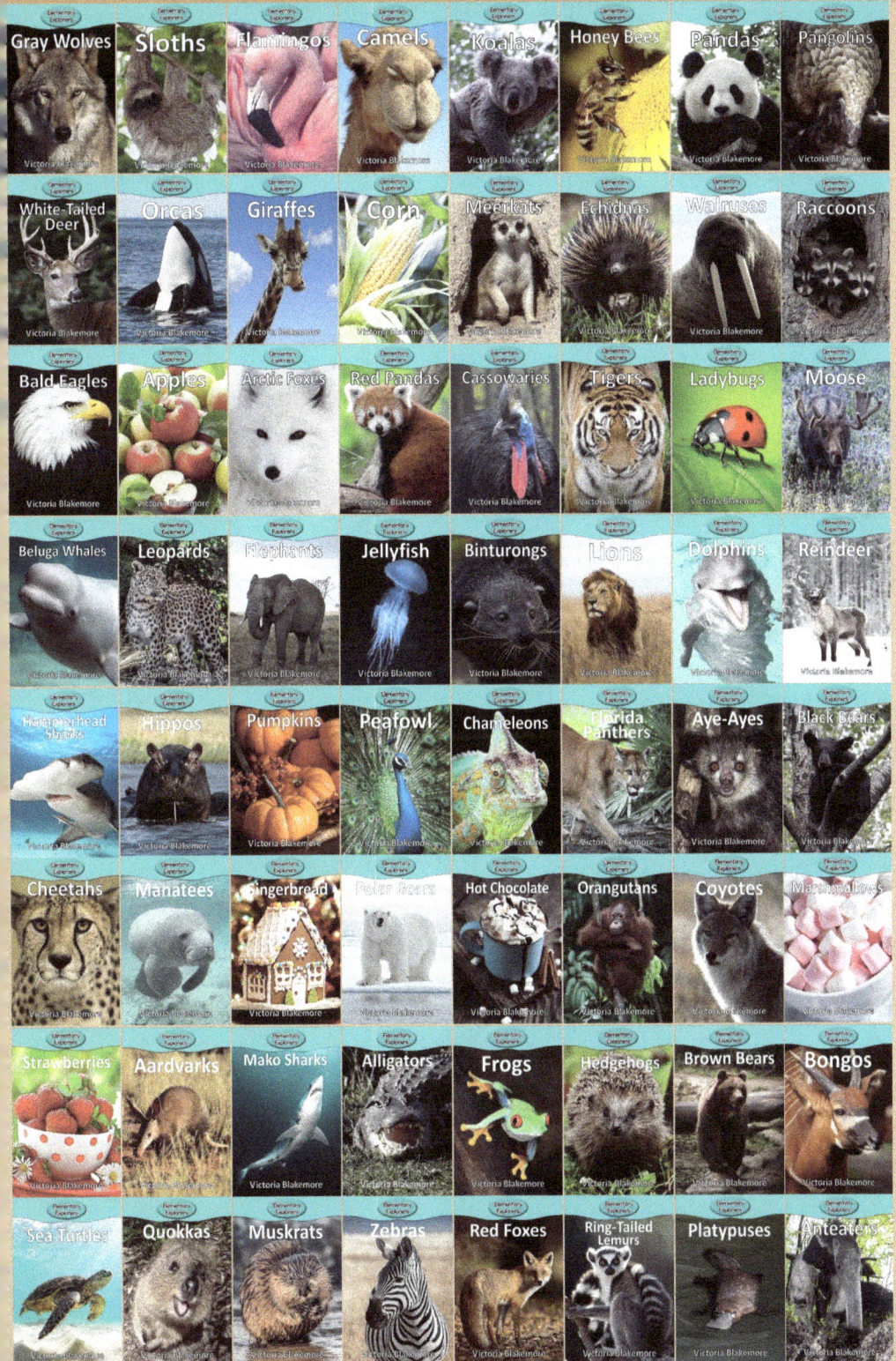

Gray Wolves	Sloths	Flamingos	Camels	Koalas	Honey Bees	Pandas	Pangolins
White-Tailed Deer	Orcas	Giraffes	Corn	Meerkats	Echidnas	Walruses	Raccoons
Bald Eagles	Apples	Arctic Foxes	Red Pandas	Cassowaries	Tigers	Ladybugs	Moose
Beluga Whales	Leopards	Elephants	Jellyfish	Binturongs	Lions	Dolphins	Reindeer
Hammerhead Sharks	Hippos	Pumpkins	Peafowl	Chameleons	Florida Panthers	Aye-Ayes	Black Bears
Cheetahs	Manatees	Gingerbread	Polar Bears	Hot Chocolate	Orangutans	Coyotes	Marshmallows
Strawberries	Aardvarks	Mako Sharks	Alligators	Frogs	Hedgehogs	Brown Bears	Bongos
Sea Turtles	Quokkas	Muskrats	Zebras	Red Foxes	Ring-Tailed Lemurs	Platypuses	Anteaters

Also in This Series

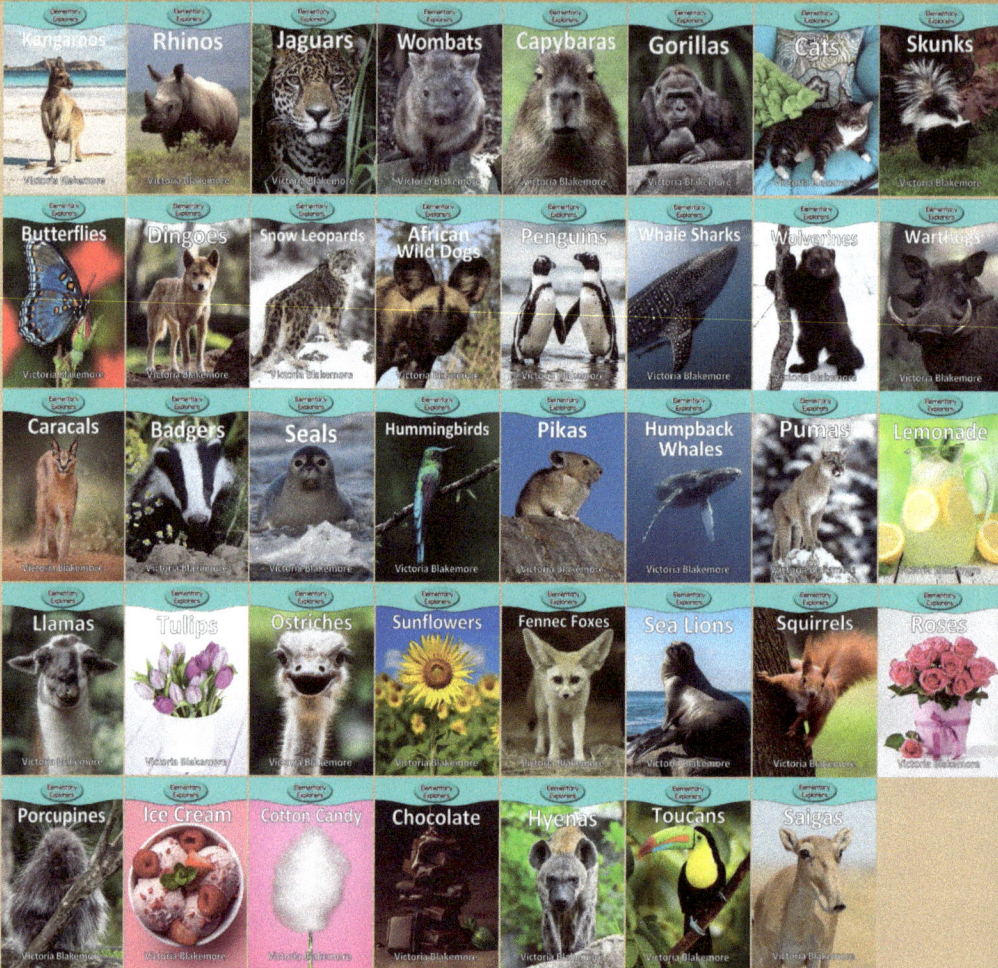

Kangaroos · Rhinos · Jaguars · Wombats · Capybaras · Gorillas · Cats · Skunks

Butterflies · Dingoes · Snow Leopards · African Wild Dogs · Penguins · Whale Sharks · Wolverines · Warthogs

Caracals · Badgers · Seals · Hummingbirds · Pikas · Humpback Whales · Pumas · Lemonade

Llamas · Tulips · Ostriches · Sunflowers · Fennec Foxes · Sea Lions · Squirrels · Roses

Porcupines · Ice Cream · Cotton Candy · Chocolate · Hyenas · Toucans · Saigas

www.ingramcontent.com/pod-product-compliance
Lightning Source LLC
Chambersburg PA
CBHW051252020426
42333CB00025B/3170